waterhouses
the romantic alternative

ferenc maté

ALBATROSS PUBLISHING HOUSE

DESIGNED BY CANDACE MATÉ

To Candace, who was nice enough
to take a week off from building our houseboat
to marry me.

It must have been the money. I probably had hordes of other excuses at the time for building—with a hand-saw and a hammer—a little house that floated on the water, but looking back as honestly as one can on such things, I now say that it must have been the money. Not that eleven years ago it was regarded as completely cheap to build a little house for $800, but when one considers that the little house had a little kitchen and a little bath and a little fireplace and little skylights and little else, along with the fact that it was moored beside a thousand acre park in the heart of Vancouver, then even the most incorrigibly frugal could not, with any conviction, call it expensive.

Even though it resembled an arrogant shoe-box, it did give me a sense of pride and I could think of nothing more magical than sitting on my aft porch dangling my feet in the harbour and watching gulls and ducks and swans and boats with crisp white sails, drift by. And the duck-quacks and the gull-screams would drown out the muffled shouts and roaring laughter of the finger-pointers who said, "Look at the madman in the floating shoe-box." But the sunshine came in from the water and danced on the walls.

The nights were quiet. The breeze would slap wavelets against the hull, not loudly, just enough to move the house and set hanging-lamps and basket-chairs and fern-pots gently swaying.

Women loved it. They liked the dark little place with things swaying. I didn't like them. Then I met someone I did like. She hated me. But she got over that during an outing to Guatemala where they have heat, and swamps, and sweat, and raindrops so heavy they leave dents in the roof of your Volkswagen bus. That took four months. I'm not an easy man to unhate.

When we got back we had nowhere to live. We had the bus and an old dying Porsche, but even if you tied the two together you still couldn't really call it a decent house. We did the only thing you can do when you need a place to live and have nothing—we built a houseboat.

It was winter. It was cold. There was frost on the telephone wires in the morning. And in the trees.

We needed some pontoons to start construction. We found four new ones, plywood with fibreglass over, but we didn't have the money. What we did have was the Porsche. It had been raced. The interior had been stripped of all lining and insulation. When you accelerated you could swear the valves were going to kick the fillings from your teeth. We traded. Four pontoons for one Porsche.

We began construction in January in False Creek in the fog. We moved aboard April Fool's Day in the sunshine. It had taken three months to build the 470 square foot floathouse with livingroom, fireplace, study, dining room, kitchen, bathroom, sleeping-loft and three outside decks. Two "Homes" magazines raved about the fine design and high quality of construction. Most of the material we used was reject.

The glass for the windows was quarter-inch tinted plate. We bought it from a man who salvaged it from a burnt-out store. We paid one third of retail. The cedar siding was reject because it had knots. We paid half of retail and cut around. The huge steel hood over the fireplace was once a cement hopper. The owner paid us seven dollars to haul it away. We needed a car to haul all the junk. We bought an ancient Morris Oxford station wagon for $170. It had leather seats and a new clutch. The next day the clutch fell all over the pavement. It hauled used bricks for the fireplace. It hauled oak for the floors. We bought flooring for half price because it had knots and worm holes. We liked those knots and holes better than the clean pink wood.

In a waterhouse you must insulate the floors. We stretched old fishnet between the floor-joists and stuffed the six inch space with reject styrofoam sheets. These are somehow cut to uneven thickness during manufacturing. We paid twenty dollars for two huge mountains of it. The fishnets never complained about the aesthetic discrepancies. We stuffed the sheets into the floor and the ceiling and the walls. The house was so soundproof you couldn't hear yourself scream. In the middle of the living room still lay a small mountain of the wretched white stuff. We had no use for it. We wrapped it in a fishnet, then I stepped through a window onto our tiny aft deck and pulled the scrap-mountain after me. It was too big. It stuck. I told Candace to push. Then I was floating on my back down False Creek with a mountain of styrofoam resting on my belly.

The propane tank was second hand, the propane stove had an eighty dollar scratch on the side that you couldn't see after it had been built in, and the hot water tank had a dent worth $39.95 plus tax. But the inside of the kitchen cabinet where the tank lived didn't care. In all, the bill of materials was $2,980. That was five years ago.

But the Morris Oxford with the leather seats and the new clutch was on its deathbed. We took it to a junkman who offered us five dollars. Then he saw the copper radiator. He gave us six.

seattle

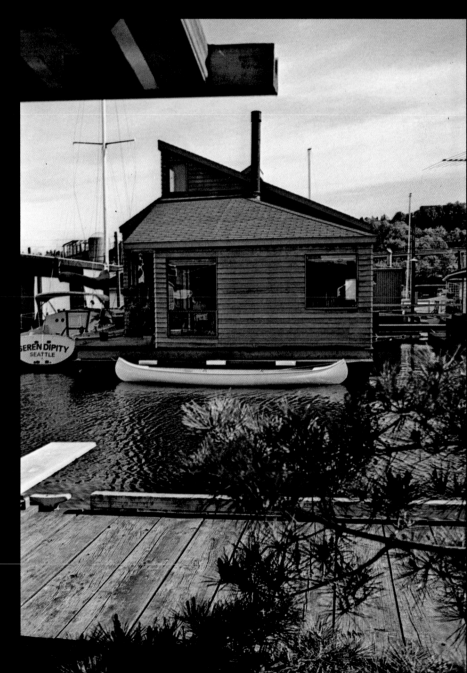

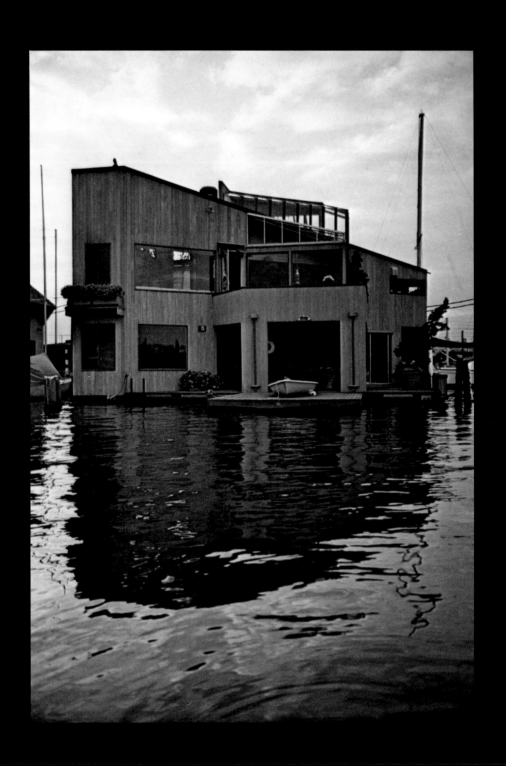

They're organized here. They have long floating streets with lamps and house numbers and trees along the floating streets, and floating gardens, and sailboats and kayaks and canoes tied behind the houses or slung in slings to keep the bottoms clean, and pet geese and pet ducks that drift among the houses and hunt for floating goodies and go "quack".

In Lake Union they're a few minutes from mid-town and a few minutes from the university and only minutes from anywhere else. They're organized. They have a yearly "luau" with a pig pit and a luau table built to such a mass that it takes twelve strong men and six hernias to move, and "stringer" parties which are mostly unplanned and can happen to any house that floats on masses of ancient cedar logs which in time get waterlogged and give up the ghost and sink. Luckily they do so one at a time causing only a temporary list until a stringer party gathers and a new log is jammed and tugged and kicked and cursed into place and then everybody's happy again and half drunk.

Most of the houses are of very good quality. Missing, is the luxurious madness of Saucilito, but the romance is here in imaginativeness and craftsmanship. It's in the tiny cottage with the cedar tub, hollowed from a solid log, and a tree as the centre-piece, and tiny rooms tucked carefully away with every square inch utilized and lovely and precious.

The romance is in a masterpiece of design that juts from the water like an angry grey rock and has inside a greenhouse and oak floors with round brass plugs instead of nails, and a desk suspended by brass rods with bronze turnbuckles for adjustment, and light pouring in everywhere from decks and skylights and water-level windows.

The romance is here at the end of the wharf in the house of a soft-spoken editor whose place is a museum of oriental nicknacks like huge brass cups from Thieves Market in Hong Kong, brass clothes racks from a dead ship of the Philippines and precious bits of ivory and teak and bronze from yachts and steamers around the world.

The romance is in the raspy voice of the pediatrician who has spent months in finishing his upstairs ceiling in fan-swirls of cedar.

"I make good money you know. I could move. I could move anywhere into anything. But why? Tell me why? Where else can I find this sense of community, this warmth, this light? Where else can I find it? Tell me where?" I can't tell him.

san francisco

They build anything on anything that floats. No laws govern houseboat construction, so there are tall ones and squat ones, thin ones and plump ones, ones that look like magic castles, others Noah's Ark, others like his dog. Some look like old riverboats, others ARE old riverboats. There are tee-pees on scows, and barns on scows, and scows on scows. Some are two-storied and stuccoed and in rows like tidy suburbs, others are being sucked down by the mud. Some are ancient and crumbling fishermen's shacks, others are jewels with copper roofs, redwood siding, stained-glass windows, $150,000 price tags, and a giant white parrot that lives in a room of his own so high his droppings take a week and a half to reach the floor below. His owner sells specialty items like whole lakes and whole islands and whole mountain tops for millions, and anything else eccentric like that, that I'd care to name. I don't. I just sit with my mouth agape and watch the parrot feeling lonely in his tower. I leave.

I'm jammed in a tiny shack. No one can remember what it was built of, or why, or when. The ceiling is so low that I have to bend my neck and stare at the floor when I talk, which makes my voice muffled and the place sound cozy. It is. I could touch both walls if I stretched out my elbows. I don't dare. The owner, standing in an overcoat of enormous bulk, despite the heat, talks feverishly of the specialty items that he sells: whole old doorknobs, and whole old bolts, and whole old nails and whole new eggs. The price is two-bits a handful. I can mix and match eggs with bolts or nails with doorknobs or any combination that I care to name. Two-bits a handful. I want to glance at his face to see if he is serious but the ceiling is pressing my chin into my Adam's apple. Water gathers around my ankles. The tide is coming in.

They build anything on anything that floats. They build on cedar logs or styrofoam blocks or old wood scows or old steel scows or new scows of ferro-cement. They build their own pontoons of plywood with fibreglass over, or tar over, or nothing over, or they buy aluminum pontoons from dead float-planes. They build on forty-five-gallon steel drums strapped together, or nine World War II navy-mines welded into a pattern. Some last for fifty years, others sink the day that they are finished. There are no laws.

If the thing doesn't quite float, that's all right too, so long as it's tall. They take tall old boats with tall old holes and ram them tight into the shallow muddy banks of Richardson's Bay where the tide doesn't change too much —just enough to wander in and out of the holes but not enough to reach the dwellers on the deck above.

When the sun goes behind the hill and the thick pale air that drips the oil of eucalyptus trees becomes pink and sparkling like Venice in early morning, and the tiny narrow bridges that link the waterhouses, sway and creak and groan on the shifting water, you sit among the bicycle wheels and the planters and the chickens, and hope it'll never change.

amsterdam

It's clean. Everything is so clean that you keep spinning your head looking for the sweepers, and the wipers, and the dusters. The air is clean and blue and you can see the end of the universe or you can count the bricks in the wall of the building across the canal if you'd rather. The trees are clean, and the thousands of ancient black bicycles that swarm like locust are clean, and the steel rails along the canals glisten, and the old canal-boats, now canal-houses, glisten, so that you are afraid to go too near in case the paint is still wet; and the lace curtains in their windows are so white that you have to squint.

The narrow canals line Amsterdam like a spider's web, and the canal-boats line the canals end to end along the narrow stone walls. They're long, some eighty feet, some more, and like the canals, narrow. Their holds, that used to house cargo, now house people, and their decks have sky-lights to let the sun pour into the narrow precious rooms with built-in cribs, and tables, and pantries, and tiny greenhouses where herbs grow. The inside of the hulls have been scraped and painted, or scraped and lined with Norwegian Pine. The original fittings are everywhere: giant, polished brass bells and copper-tubes sparkle and decorate and act as places for pots to hang or plants to climb. Teak grates that were once for cargo, are scraped and sanded and oiled and glow richly as partition screens or table tops or book shelves. On deck, are piles of fire-wood and garden chairs and rows of flower pots and everywhere, an ancient black bicycle. The woodwork of varnished teak that was the old wheelhouse, shines, and kids crawl about in the sun. Some barges kept their engine in fine repair so that they can untie and move on, on whim or need.

Near the heart of town a canal is lined with flower barges. They'll sell you cut flowers or whole flowers, and bulbs and seeds and roots and pots and shrubs and little tools that dig and little plants that wilt when you touch them or ones that eat flys and smell like dog-breath. At night the flower boats are closed but strings of tiny light-bulbs bathe everything with a million tiny moons. The silent black-green water reflects and makes it two.

Outside the city, canal-houses line the low banks under willows and stone bridges and windmills. Dairy cows roam the endless flat green fields. There's more to

see than skylights alone allow, so many have built structures atop the barges with huge clean windows looking onto huge green views and long lace curtains so white you have to squint.

london

Down in Chelsea, not far from the Chelsea bridge, about a two stone's throw if you have a good arm, six if you don't, below the stone-wall-lined banks of the thick, brown Thames, are rows of barge-boats that roam no more. They're tied to the wall and to each other, all with new structures built upon the old barges below.

In early summer, when the Thames churns high, women with full breasts that glow winter-white, lie uncovered on the hot wood decks trying to change colour. Tall red buses cross the bridge but the wind keeps their sounds away. Ropes creak gently, wind-chimes softly sound, and everything moves and swings, just a little, just enough so that you never forget that you are on water. A man in a peaked grey cap leans on the iron rail of his barge and sometimes stares at his fishing pole, but most times at the white breasts pinking. When the wind comes up, the Thames ruffles, and a jillion tiny suns sparkle into your eyes.

Back upriver a narrow green island splits the Thames in two. On one side, a one-car bridge connects it to the road and park and houses; on the other, the river flows uncrossed between the tiny island and tree-lined pastures. A grassy path forms the island's spine and on either side are miniature fenced gardens with roses and lilacs and radishes and tulips and tomatoes and rippled-leaved currant bushes, and at the bottom of the gardens flows the Thames and upon it floats each garden's house.

The houses, like the gardens, are simple; most are on old wood scows, some on old barge-boat hulls, most single storied, some double, but no two are alike.

The lady with the stone-firm voice, who lives beside the bridge, will tell you all the island's history, about the barges and the problems and the beauty and the changes and the old music hall queen who lives on the island's tip in a powder blue waterhouse that cost thirty-thousand pounds to renovate and more to decorate, and about the gas lamps that line the paths, and about her old dog that she must constantly keep an eye on because he's senile and tends to walk off the gang-plank into the Thames and go splash and sink without a gurgle.

vancouver

backwaters